A personal tribute from Archbishop Desmond Tutu, close friend of Nelson Mandela.

I first met Nelson Mandela (Madiba) in the 1950s when he adjudicated our college debating contest. We didn't meet again until the day he was released from prison in 1990.

Madiba was never angry or complained about his twenty-seven years in prison. He believed in peace, and he taught us all an essential lesson about forgiveness when he invited his former prison guard to be a guest at his election as President of South Africa.

He cared deeply about people and worked hard to set up charities and raise funds to build a better future for South Africa. Madiba believed children were a huge part of that future, and contributed from his salary to set up the Nelson Mandela Children's Fund. So it is wonderful that this book exists for children to share in the story of his inspiring life.

One of my fondest memories of Madiba is how funny he was. I once made fun of the bright, colourful shirts he wore and he replied that at least he didn't wear a dress in public, like me.

Our world is a better place for having had a Nelson Mandela. He has taught us so much about understanding and respecting each other for our differences. He was amazing, and I feel blessed that he was my friend.

Johannesburg, South Africa, March 2014

The Nelson Mandela Foundation is thanked for its support and advice.

First published 2009 by Macmillan Children's Books
This edition published 2014 by Macmillan Children's Books
a division of Macmillan Publishers Limited
20 New Wharf Road, London N1 9RR
Basingstoke and Oxford
Associated companies throughout the world
www.panmacmillan.com

ISBN: 978-1-4772-7554-1

Illustrations by Paddy Bouma
Text abridged by Chris van Wyk

Abridged from the book LONG WALK TO FREEDOM by Nelson Mandela
Copyright © Nelson Rolihlahla Mandela 1994

This abridgement and illustrations copyright © Macmillan 2009
Image on page 3 courtesy of the Nelson Mandela Foundation & Oryx Media
Image on page 7 courtesy of Tom Stoddart Archive, Getty Images
The illustrator would like to thank Carin Matz for the use of her photograph on which the illustration
on page 53 is based, and also the Mayibuye Centre for their help with image research.

1 3 5 7 9 8 6 4 2

A CIP catalogue record for this book is available from the British Library.

Printed in China

NELSON MANDELA
LONG WALK to FREEDOM

ABRIDGED BY CHRIS VAN WYK
ILLUSTRATED BY PADDY BOUMA

Macmillan Children's Books

AFRICA

SOUTH
AFRICA

BOTSWANA

LIMPOPO

PRETORIA

JOHANNESBURG

SOWETO   GAUTENG   ALEXANDRA

NORTH WEST   MPUMALANGA

SWAZILAND

NAMIBIA

FREE STATE

KWAZULU-
NATAL

BLOEMFONTEIN

LESOTHO   HOWICK
DURBAN

SOUTH AFRICA

NORTHERN CAPE

UMTATA

CLARKEBURY
SCHOOL   QUNU

EASTERN CAPE   MVEZO

MQHEKEZWENI

FORT BEAUFORT
HEALDTOWN
COLLEGE   EAST LONDON

UNIVERSITY OF
FORT HARE

WESTERN CAPE

ROBBEN ISLAND   CAPE TOWN

POLLSMOOR PRISON   PORT ELIZABETH

My name is Nelson Mandela. I live in South Africa, a beautiful country on the tip of Africa. Today South Africa is a democracy. That means all adults vote to choose who they want to run the country. But it was not always like this. When I was born, South Africa was ruled by white people only. As I grew older I began to see that this was not fair. I wanted to change this way of government so everyone had a say. My friends and I called this the struggle for freedom. The struggle lasted many years and I was one of the fighters. This is my story . . .

Long, long ago, white Europeans crossed the seas to South Africa. They fought over the land, and they also fought the tribes of people already living there, such as the Xhosas, the Zulus and the Tswanas.

Hundreds of years later, I was born into the Thembu tribe, one of many tribes that made up the Xhosa nation. I entered the world in the tiny village of Mvezo, in the beautiful Eastern Cape, on 18th July, 1918.

My father was a Thembu chief, a leader of our people. He named me Rolihlahla, which in Xhosa means "troublemaker". Did he believe I would grow up to be a troublemaker? I don't think so. Nobody knew what lay ahead of me.

When I was a young boy, we moved from Mvezo to the nearby village of Qunu and I began herding our family's sheep and goats. Those were happy days. My friends and I swam in the rivers, stole honey from beehives, and played stick-fighting — a Xhosa boy's favourite sport.

When I turned seven, my father decided to send me to school. It was a mission school, built by Europeans who had come to South Africa to spread Christianity. No one in my family had been to school before. I didn't have fancy clothes but my father took a pair of his old trousers and cut them off at the knee. I used a piece of string as a belt. But the school wasn't fancy, either — it had only one classroom. None of the pupils wore smart clothes, so I fitted right in.

Our teacher gave us new names. Mine was Nelson. Nelson? At that time the English ruled our country, so our teacher thought we should all have English names. It sounded very strange at first, but I soon got used to it.

I was learning at school but I was learning at home as well. My mother told me stories from long ago, full of wise lessons about being kind to others.

My father taught me to be a brave Xhosa boy. I wanted to grow up to be just like him. Sometimes I even rubbed ash onto my hair to make it grey, like his.

But after my ninth birthday, my life changed. My father grew ill and died. My mother took me to live with my father's friend, Chief Jongintaba, in the nearby village of Mqhekezweni. Uncle Jongi was the acting king of the Thembus and was a very important man. He had a motor car and lived in a big house called the Great Place. It was an exciting new experience for me! My mother still came to visit me though and I was always happy to see her.

Although I missed Qunu, I loved my new life. Uncle Jongi's son, Justice, was a few years older than me and we became best friends. We rode horses and ploughed his father's fields together. We had a lot of fun!

But life was not all about riding horses. When I was 16, Uncle Jongi sent me to Clarkebury boarding school. In those days many boys and girls did not finish their schooling, but my uncle believed education was important. Three years later, I joined Justice at Healdtown, the biggest school for Africans in the country. This is where I completed my high school education.

At the age of 21, I enrolled at Fort Hare,
a university for black students in the
Eastern Cape. Uncle Jongi bought me a new
suit to wear. It was very different from
the cut-down trousers I had worn when
I went to school. I felt very grown-up!

Young black people from all over the
country came to study at Fort Hare. It was
the first time I had met people from other
tribes, such as Sothos, Zulus and Tswanas.

I made new friends, including a clever
young student called Oliver Tambo.
Although we didn't know it then, Oliver
and I were to become very important
in each other's lives.

I worked hard at university but I had fun, too. I took up running, boxing and ballroom dancing. One night, my friends and I snuck out to a dance-hall. We thought we were very daring — until we met our teacher! But suddenly my student days were cut short. I was elected to sit on the Student Council, but only 25 students had voted. Most did not vote because the Council could not change the thing that concerned them the most — the bad canteen food. I told the Principal that I would not sit on the Council without the students' support. He was very angry and threatened to expel me, but I wouldn't change my mind. I never went back to university. Was I living up to my name of "troublemaker"?

Back at the Great Place, Uncle Jongi soon had other plans for me and Justice. He told us we were to be married, and he had already picked a wife for each of us. We were shocked! We didn't want to get married and so we decided to run away to Johannesburg.

Johannesburg was over 700 kilometres away. It was known to all Xhosa people as Egoli, the Place of Gold. There we would find jobs and make new lives. It was an adventure, and we set off full of hope and excitement for the future, towards the twinkling lights of the big city.

The city was bigger than we could ever have imagined. Everywhere we looked there were people, shops and cars. But those smart shops and expensive cars belonged to white people. Most black people were poor.

I went to live in Alexandra township, just outside the city, where the tiny houses had no electricity or running water and the roads were just dusty paths. Life was hard in Alexandra, but it became home to me.

Justice stayed in Johannesburg for a while. But after a few years Uncle Jongi died and Justice returned to the Eastern Cape to take over as chief.

I met many new people but one of my best friends was Walter Sisulu. Walter and his family lived in Orlando West, Soweto, a black township near Johannesburg. I looked up to Walter. Like me, he was from the Eastern Cape but he had been in Johannesburg longer and knew a lot about the city's people and places.

I spent a lot of time at the Sisulus' home. It was there I met Evelyn Mase, a young nurse and relative of the Sisulus. We fell in love and got married. We had two sons and two daughters, but one daughter did not live long. Sadly, Evelyn and I soon parted, but I remained close to my sons, Thembekile and Makgatho, and to my daughter, Makaziwe.

At the Sisulus' I also met my old friend Oliver Tambo again. We were both studying law and in 1952 we set up the first black law firm in South Africa.

MANDELA AND TAMBO

But there was another way we could try to improve the lives of black people. Ever since white people had come to South Africa, they had ruled black people. My friend Walter was a member of the African National Congress, or ANC, which had been fighting for the freedom of black people to rule themselves. Oliver and I joined too and, at Walter's home, we wondered how we could make the government take notice.

In 1944 we formed the ANC Youth League and planned to get thousands of young black people to join. We would protest peacefully by marching through the streets and demanding our freedom. We would not be ignored.

In 1948 the government started passing laws that introduced apartheid, which divided black and white people into separate groups. White people lived in suburbs while black people lived in townships. The government also built separate schools, churches and cinemas for black and for white people. There were even separate entrances to post offices and shops.

All black people over 16 years of age had to carry a passbook showing who we were, and where we worked and lived. If we were found without our passbook, we would be thrown into prison.

Apartheid was a cruel system. It classified
every person in South Africa according to
race, for example as "black", "coloured"
or "white", and controlled the lives of those
who were not white. It made me and my ANC
comrades angry. In 1952 we led a protest
called the Defiance Campaign, calling on black
people to ignore the "Whites Only" entrances
in post offices, shops and trains. Over 250
people were arrested but thousands joined in.

The government didn't drop its apartheid
laws, but the ANC now had many more
members. We were getting stronger. The
government banned me from attending ANC
meetings or protesting against apartheid,
but I went on working for the ANC in secret.

It was not only black people who were against apartheid. Thousands of Coloured, Indian and white South Africans were against it too. In the early 1950s, many of these different groups joined together to form the Congress Alliance. Then, in 1955, the ANC and the other members of the Congress Alliance met in Kliptown, near Johannesburg, to draw up the Freedom Charter. The meeting was called the Congress of the People, and the Charter was a promise to fight for freedom and democracy for all South Africans. It began . . .

THE FREEDOM CHARTER

We the people of South Africa, declare for all our country and the world to know :- That South Africa belongs to all who live in it, black and white . . .

The government did not like the Charter and arrested 156 Congress members, including Oliver, Walter and me. We were charged with planning to destroy the government. The trial lasted four long years but in the end we were found not guilty.

During that time, I fell in love again. Winnie Madikizela was a social worker, and a member of the ANC. We got married in 1958 and had two daughters, Zenani and Zindzi.

In 1960, during our trial, a tragedy happened that shocked the world.

In Sharpeville, near Johannesburg, 5,000 people marched to a police station to protest against having to carry passbooks. They were not armed, yet still the police fired guns at them.

Sixty-nine people were killed and 400 were injured.

After Sharpeville, the government banned
the ANC and other organisations fighting
for freedom. They did not want to share
South Africa with black people. Our
peaceful marches had not worked, but we
were not giving up. We decided that the
only way to get our freedom was to fight
the government in the same way as they
were fighting us — with guns.

The ANC formed an army which we called
Umkhonto we Sizwe, which in Xhosa means
"The Spear of the Nation". I was sent
abroad on a secret mission to ask other
countries to help us fight apartheid.
I also went to train as a soldier.

In 1962 I returned to South Africa, using a false passport and calling myself David Motsamayi. I stayed in hiding for many months while the police searched everywhere for Nelson Mandela . . .

Then, one day in August, I was stopped in my car and arrested. I was sentenced to five years in prison for leaving the country illegally and for inciting workers to strike. Later the police also arrested a group of my comrades, including my old friend Walter Sisulu. Just nine months into my five year sentence, I was told I would stand trial again. We were all charged with planning to overthrow the government. If we were found guilty, we could be sentenced to death.

The trial began in October 1963, and in April 1964 I spoke in defence of us all. I told the court that the ANC was a peaceful organisation, but because the government had banned it, we had no peaceful way to protest. We had been imprisoned and even killed. This is why we had to fight back with guns. I said, "I have cherished the ideal of a democracy in which all persons live together in harmony . . . It is an ideal for which I am prepared to die."

Eight of us were found guilty, but we were not sentenced to death. Instead, we were told we would spend the rest of our lives in prison. Life in prison! Would I ever see my wife, mother and children again?

We were taken to Robben Island, a prison off the coast of Cape Town. All except our comrade Denis Goldberg. Of the eight of us, he was the only white person and had to serve his sentence at a different prison.

On Robben Island, my cell was so tiny that when I lay down on my sleeping mat, my feet and hands could touch opposite walls. I was given some thin blankets and a bucket for a toilet. This cell was to be my home.

I tried to stay hopeful but it wasn't easy. At first we were allowed only two visitors a year, and just two letters. Before we were given them, the letters were read by a prison guard who blacked out anything he thought we shouldn't know about.

Twice I received bad news from home. First, I was told my mother had died. Then my eldest son, Thembekile, was killed in a car crash. When I got that news I spent the whole day in my cell thinking about him and the rest of my family. It was one of the saddest days of my life.

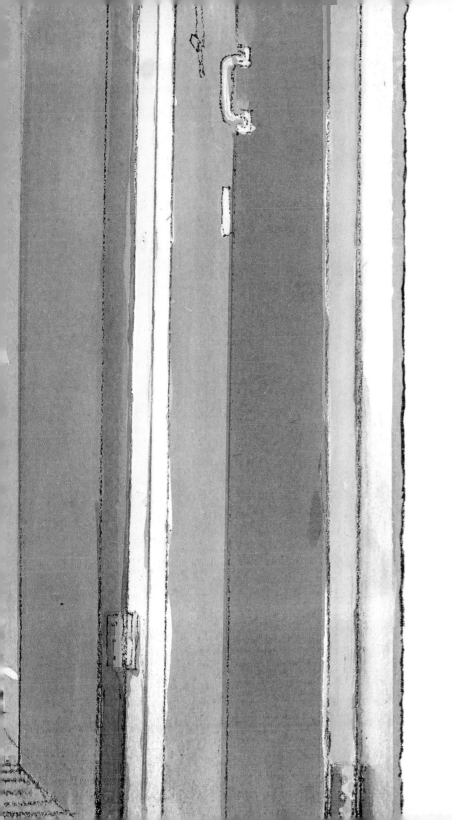

We were not allowed radios or newspapers. Weeks, months, years went by without us knowing what was happening in the world. One day, I saw that a warder had left his newspaper lying on a chair. It was too tempting. I grabbed the paper and began reading it. I was caught and locked in a room for three days with no food and only rice water to drink as a punishment.

Slowly the years passed. Five years . . . ten . . . twenty. I no longer needed ash to make my hair grey!

But outside the prison, the fight for freedom went on.

Even though the ANC was banned in South Africa, it continued outside the country. Oliver Tambo was living abroad and was now ANC president. Many governments around the world began to support us.

In the 1980s the ANC launched the "Release Mandela" campaign, asking people all over the world to put pressure on the South African government to release me and my fellow prisoners, and to allow the ANC back in. Thousands of people signed the petition.

Then, in March 1982, Walter, a few other prisoners and I were moved to Pollsmoor prison near Cape Town. Was this a sign that things were beginning to change? Should I dare to hope our struggle for freedom was coming to an end? The government and I began secret talks about peace.

In 1988 I was moved again to a prison called Victor Verster, but instead of a cell, I was given a cottage with a bedroom, a kitchen and a swimming pool!

The government and I continued our talks, and in December 1989 I met with President de Klerk and we talked about a new South Africa. Things began to move very quickly.

Back in October 1989 a number of my former Robben Island comrades had been released, including Walter Sisulu. Then, on 2nd February 1990 and two months after our meeting, President de Klerk stunned the world by announcing that I was to be released, along with all other political prisoners. He said it was time to talk about a new country.

On 11th February 1990 I walked out of prison. Twenty-seven years of my life had passed since I was first taken to Robben Island. But the long walk to freedom was almost over.

It was wonderful to hold my lovely wife Winnie in my arms, to see my four beautiful children — now grown up, and to hear my grandchildren laugh and call me Granddad!

Every day our Soweto home was filled with laughter and tears of joy as friends I hadn't seen in twenty-seven years came to welcome me home.

After our release, there was a lot of work to be done. The ANC and the government began to speak about peace, and about a South Africa that would be shared by all its people, black and white . . .

And on 27th April 1994 millions of people, young and old, streamed out of their homes to vote. It was the first time ever for black people, and they joined white people to vote for a new South Africa. It was a wonderful day!

In May 1994 I became the first president of South Africa to be elected by all the people.

I was 75 years old. My journey to freedom had ended.

But a new journey has now begun — a journey to build a new South Africa.

We must join hands and say we are one country, one nation,

one people, marching together into the future.

A future in which people of all colours will

learn to live in peace.

Nelson Mandela was President of South Africa for five years. True to his promise to only serve one term, he stepped down as President in 1999, though he continued to work with leaders of other countries to try and make the world a better place for all. He also set up the Nelson Mandela Children's Fund, the Nelson Mandela Foundation and The Mandela Rhodes Foundation.

Every year the world celebrates Nelson Mandela International Day on 18th July — his birthday. People mark the day by spending at least 67 minutes doing something for others. Each minute represents one of the 67 years that Nelson Mandela spent fighting for freedom and peace.

Nelson Mandela passed away on 5th December 2013, aged 95. But his memory lives on as an inspiration to us all to believe in a world where nobody should suffer oppression or poverty.

TIMELINE

1918   Nelson Mandela is born
at Mvezo on July 18th
and named Rolihlahla

1925   Goes to a Methodist
mission school.
Renamed Nelson by his teacher

1930   His father, Henry Gadla Mphakanyiswa, dies.
Mandela goes to live with
Chief Jongintaba Dalindyebo

1934   Goes to Clarkebury Boarding Institute

1937   Goes to Healdtown, the Wesleyan College at
Fort Beaufort

1939   Enrols at
University College
of Fort Hare

1940   Leaves Fort Hare after refusing
to sit on the Student Council

1941   Runs away to Johannesburg

1944   Joins the ANC and helps to form the
Youth League.
Marries Evelyn Mase

1948   National Party elected and begins
introducing apartheid laws

1952   Opens South Africa's first black
law firm with Oliver Tambo.
The ANC and the SAIC launch
the Defiance Campaign

1955   The Freedom Charter is drawn up
at the Congress of the People

1956   Mandela is charged with treason
along with 155 others.
Four-year court case begins

1958   Divorces Evelyn Mase.
Marries Winnie Madikizela

1960   Sharpeville massacre.
The government bans the ANC

1961   Treason trial ends. Mandela
is found not guilty.
The ANC forms an army

1962   Mandela is sent to get support
from other countries.
Arrested again on his return to South Africa.
Sentenced to five years for leaving the
country illegally and inciting workers
to strike

1963   Nine months into his sentence, Mandela is told he will stand trial again

1964   Found guilty of sabotage, along with Walter Sisulu, Ahmed Kathrada, Raymond Mhlaba, Govan Mbeki, Denis Goldberg, Elias Motsoaledi and Andrew Mlangeni. Sentenced to life in prison and sent to Robben Island

1969   Mandela's son, Thembekile, dies in a car accident

1980-2   Thousands of people sign the "Release Mandela" petition

1982   Mandela is moved to Pollsmoor Prison

1988   Moved to Victor Verster prison

1989   Five of the men who were convicted alongside Mandela are released: Sisulu, Kathrada, Mhlaba, Motsoaledi and Mlangeni. (Goldberg had been released earlier in 1985, and Mbeki in 1987)

1990   Mandela is released from prison

1994   Votes for the first time in his life in South Africa's first democratic election. Elected as President of South Africa

1995   Establishes the Nelson Mandela Children's Fund

1996   Divorces Winnie Madikizela-Mandela

1998   Marries Graça Machel on his 80th birthday

1999   Steps down as President of South Africa. Establishes the Nelson Mandela Foundation

2003   Establishes the Mandela Rhodes Foundation

2004   Announces his retirement from public life

2009   First Nelson Mandela International Day is celebrated on 18th July in honour of his birthday

2013   Nelson Mandela passes away on 5th December, aged 95

GLOSSARY

adjudicated – acted as a judge and referee

African National Congress (ANC) – an organisation formed in 1912 by those who believed that all Africans should be free to vote to choose their own leaders. The ANC led the fight to end apartheid

apartheid – a system, introduced in 1948, that classified and separated black, Coloured and Indian people from white people in South Africa. Under the laws of apartheid only white people could vote, and the lives of black people were strictly controlled. The word apartheid means "apartness"

charter – a document which states a group's ideas, beliefs and demands

comrades – a word sometimes used to describe people who share the same ideas and beliefs

Congress of the People – a group of different organisations that met in Kliptown, Johannesburg, in 1955 to write down their beliefs and demands for a new South Africa. The groups included the ANC, representatives from the white COD (the Congress of Democrats), Indian people from the SAIC (South African Indian Congress) and people from the SACPO (South African Coloured People's Organisation). The Freedom Charter was agreed to at the Congress of the People

De Klerk – Frederik Willem de Klerk was president of South Africa from 1989 to 1994. In 1990 he ended the ban on the ANC and ordered the release of Mandela. Under his leadership, the government reversed the last of the apartheid laws. F.W. de Klerk and Mandela were awarded the Nobel Peace Prize in 1993

debating – to have a discussion about a particular subject with two opposing sides

elected – to get the most votes of all the people standing for a position

government – a political group who are in power and run a country

inciting – to strongly encourage someone to do something

legacy – something left behind or handed down by somebody

Mandela Rhodes Foundation, The – a programme dedicated to educating young African leaders of the future

Nelson Mandela Children's Fund – an organisation which helps improve the lives of children

Nelson Mandela Foundation – an organisation which promotes the beliefs and work of Nelson Mandela

overthrow – to defeat or destroy

petition – a written request that is signed by all those who agree with it

political prisoners – people who have been put into prison for fighting against or disagreeing with the government

protest – to object strongly to something

sabotage – to deliberately damage something

township – an area set aside in South African cities for black people to live. White people lived in the richer suburbs

trial – the hearing of a case in court

tribe – a group of people with a shared language and culture, often from the same area

warder – a person who works in a prison

Xhosa nation – a group made up of many different tribes who have lived in the south-eastern region of South Africa since at least the eleventh century, and who speak the same language